MAYMONT

An American Estate

text by
Dale Cyrus Wheary

MAYMONT, RICHMOND, VIRGINIA

ACKNOWLEDGMENT

Maymont: An American Estate was made
possible through the very generous donation of
Nell and Hunter Thompson.

DEDICATION

This publication is dedicated to the volunteers, board members, donors, and staff,
both past and present, who have worked diligently together to preserve Maymont and offer all of
its abundant and diverse historic and natural resources for the
enjoyment and education of the public.

CONTRIBUTING STAFF AND ADVISERS

Key Maymont staff who have contributed to the production of this
book include: Kathy Alcaine, Norman Burns, Anne Du Bois, Kathy Garrett-Cox,
Nancy Lowden, Leah Moebs, Carla Murray, Fred Murray, Keri Ragland, Cathie Rosenberg,
Peggy Singlemann, Armistead Wellford, Dale Cyrus Wheary, and Evelyn Zak.
The editorial assistance of Mary Lynn Bayliss, Charles E. Brownell, Calder Loth,
Stacy Moore, Kelly O'Keefe, Elizabeth O'Leary, and
other advisers is greatly appreciated.

CONTENTS

7   Welcome to Maymont

11 Maymont, A Gilded Age Showplace

14   James and Sallie Dooley

21   The Maymont Mansion

38   Domestic Workplace

45   Estate Landscape and Gardens

58   Estate Buildings

65   From Private Residence to Public Museum and Park

69 Maymont Today

80 Maymont Estate Map

Welcome to Maymont

Everyone who visits Maymont falls in love with its special charms and the wonderful experiences it offers, from afternoons of quiet daydreams to outings full of learning and adventure. When I arrive at the estate each day, I am reminded of the generations before me who have appreciated its timeless beauty, and I am surrounded by a whole new generation making memories here. As I walk in the shade of stately outbuildings, it is easy to imagine being transported through time. So much looks the same as it did a century ago, the inspiring creation of a couple in love with each other and with art, nature, architecture, and their community. It is this love of community that has shaped Maymont into the extraordinary gift we enjoy today.

The hundred-acre property was first given by James Dooley to his wife, Sallie, as they embarked on the development of their grand estate. Three decades later, the Dooleys bequeathed their magnificent home to the Richmond community to enjoy as a museum and park. And in the ensuing decades, the Dooleys' legacy has inspired similar acts of generosity to preserve, enhance, and celebrate Maymont. Half a million guests, from near and

far and across all social and economic boundaries, now visit each year to stroll through the gardens, tour the mansion, take a carriage ride, watch otters play, pet a farm animal, or picnic on the lawn with friends and family.

As Paul Farmer, retired CEO of the American Planning Association, said, "Maymont's beauty lies partly in its ability to be different things to different people. For some it's a refuge, a place of contemplation. For others it's a place of enchantment, and for still others, it's a place of discovery and exploration."

In addition to its reputation as a community gathering place and cultural attraction, Maymont has been recognized nationally for its significance. In recent years, it has received numerous accolades and awards, including designation as one of America's Top Ten Great Public Spaces by the American Planning Association; the Ross Merrill Award for Outstanding Commitment to the Preservation and Care of Collections presented jointly by Heritage Preservation and the American Institute for Conservation of Historic and Artistic Works (AIC); and prestigious grants from the National Endowment for the Humanities (NEH) and the Institute of Museum and Library Services (IMLS).

Many passionate donors have made possible the estate's preservation and improvement as a public attraction, and since 1975, the care and management of the estate have been overseen by the nonprofit Maymont Foundation in a successful public-private partnership with the property's owner, the City of Richmond. The foundation staff, board of directors, and hundreds of dedicated volunteers have worked together to accomplish both everyday tasks as well as major projects for the benefit of the estate and its guests.

Our mission—to preserve and celebrate Maymont for the pleasure and education of everyone—is honored year-round with special events and programs, from plant sales and holiday traditions to in-depth tours and workshops. Proceeds from those activities help with ongoing maintenance and conservation, but the vast majority of funding comes from individual, foundation, and corporate donations. Every donated dollar makes it a little easier for us to share Maymont—Richmond's jewel on the James River—with thousands of guests today and for generations to come.

Through this book, we present the story of Maymont, including the generosity and vision of the Dooleys, the fascinating era in which they lived, and the treasures and natural beauty of their extraordinary gift.

NORMAN O. BURNS II
Executive Director, Maymont Foundation

Maymont, A Gilded Age Showplace

We spent such a delightful evening at Major Dooley's beautiful home "Maymont." It is really a show place. There is much natural beauty about it, situated on the banks of the James, commanding a lovely view of the river. There are wonderful Japanese gardens and wooded lands, and a driveway of five and a half miles extending over the grounds. It was just like a fairyland and, after walking all round and getting the different beautiful views in the distance, we found the Victoria waiting to take us for a drive. The sunset was glorious from the top of the hill and at dusk we went into the house and enjoyed seeing the various works of art, which the Major and his wife have collected in their extensive travels abroad. . . . I greatly enjoyed it all and their cordial hospitality.

—ETTA DONNAN MANN
Wife of William Hodges Mann, Governor of Virginia
November 16, 1912[1]

For more than a hundred years guests have marveled at Maymont's panorama of towers, glittering interiors, colorful gardens, and magnificent trees. Created as the home of James Henry Dooley (1841–1922) and Sarah O. (Sallie) May Dooley (1846–1925), Maymont is a remarkably intact example of the showplace estates that flourished in the United States at the turn of the twentieth century. Its elaborate landscape, architectural complex, and treasure-filled mansion—with its large domestic staff, latest household conveniences, and lavish social affairs—express the pinnacle of financial success, fashionable living, and modern design in the late 1880s and 1890s. Moreover, it reflects the tastes and interests of a cultivated Richmond couple in the mainstream of the times. While many estates of the era have been altered or destroyed, Maymont endures as a valuable window into the Gilded Age, an ambitious time of growing affluence, expanding American presence on the world stage, technological innovation, and heightened activity in all fields of design.[2]

Opposite: Restoration of the mansion's ornamental lawn was one of several historic landscape projects at Maymont sponsored by the Garden Club of Virginia.

Above: This view from the mid-1930s shows Maymont as it looked soon after it was bequeathed to the City of Richmond by Mrs. Dooley in 1925. The estate's significant architectural and landscape elements remain virtually unchanged today.

Right: The Italian Garden, 1923.

The American country estate, a particular genius of the Gilded Age (circa 1873–1918), was a clear demonstration of the immense wealth that was generated during a period of great economic expansion. As the legendary fortunes of American tycoons such as Vanderbilt and Rockefeller grew, so too did those of many second-tier financiers and business leaders. In 1892 the *New York Tribune Monthly* named 4,047 millionaires in the United States.[3] Among them was James H. Dooley. Building grand estates gave members of the affluent class an opportunity to create their own private domains, ideal worlds removed from increasingly crowded urban centers. Like most country places of the time, the Dooleys' one-hundred-acre estate was not agricultural but purely ornamental in intent.

The Japanese Garden, circa 1925.

Gilded Age tycoons not only shared a passion for building lavish dwellings, but they also led a surge in philanthropy, a trend to which Maymont owes its survival. The Dooleys bequeathed their estate to the City of Richmond for use as a museum and park, a gift that contributed to a national movement to make American cities more beautiful and culturally enriched. With the passage of time, Maymont became increasingly valuable as an historic resource. Its development by a single generation of one family over a thirty-year period and, thereafter, its continuous use as a museum and park helped to ensure its preservation. The estate was designated a Virginia Historic Landmark and listed on the National Register of Historic Places in 1971. Today, Maymont continues to offer enjoyment and inspiration to hundreds of thousands of people, both as a Gilded Age estate and as an expansive open space and educational facility in the heart of Virginia's capital city.

The Gilded Age estate created by James and Sallie Dooley ranks among the nation's most intact expressions of the era's eclectic tastes. Their meticulously preserved mansion is a treasure house of decorative arts shown in their original context. The grounds are enjoyed by hundreds of thousands of people who regularly stroll this bucolic haven of remarkable diversity where they experience unfolding images of the past.

—CALDER LOTH
Senior Architectural Historian, Virginia Department of Historic Resources

JAMES AND SALLIE DOOLEY

The stories, ideals, and aspirations of James and Sallie Dooley embody much of the prevailing culture of their time. Over the course of their lives, they witnessed dramatic social, economic, and technological changes, many of which are reflected in their Richmond home. And what is more, they helped to shape their time and left a lasting legacy.

James was the son of John and Sarah Dooley, Irish immigrants who settled in Richmond in the 1830s. His father established the largest hat manufacturing company in the South. A well-liked civic leader, John Dooley also founded the Montgomery Guard, Company C of the First Virginia Infantry Regiment, a volunteer militia company comprised chiefly of Irish Richmonders. As a youth, James excelled in his studies and aspired to make a fortune. Inside the cover of his Latin dictionary, he wrote, "When I have $5,178,360, I will stop making money."[4] He graduated first in his class from Georgetown College (now Georgetown University in Washington, D.C.) in 1860. Soon

Left: Sallie May Dooley as she appeared around 1869, in a miniature on ivory, painted by H.S. Loux.

Right: James Henry Dooley, 1874.

The silver academic medals James Dooley received at Georgetown College were among his most prized possessions. His classical education, analytical ability, and oratorical skills honed at Georgetown had an enduring influence on his character and his success.

after the Civil War began, he enlisted in the Confederate Army. Within one month, however, he was wounded and captured at the Battle of Williamsburg. His younger brother, John E. Dooley, led Company C in Pickett's Charge, was wounded, and imprisoned.[5] After the war, James completed a master's degree at Georgetown and, despite postwar turmoil, established a successful law practice in Richmond.[6]

The promising young attorney married the fair-haired belle Sallie May in 1869. Using the opportunity of their honeymoon to conduct business in Chicago, James wrote to his mother, "I am afraid that Sallie does not enjoy this part of her trip very much," yet he went on to state, "I am going to make a fresh start and hope to make some money."[7]

In the 1870s James Dooley served three terms in the Virginia General Assembly. Early in the next decade he began to focus principally on his growing business interests. While the American economy was experiencing unprecedented growth, the South was adapting to a new social, economic, and political order. Rebuilding the railroads that had been devastated during the Civil War was vital for the region's recovery, and to this economic sector he chose to devote his energies. With a close circle of Richmond associates, Major Dooley, as he was

Maymont serves as a window on to a pivotal time in the history of the South and of the nation. While the Colonial era and the Civil War are well represented in Virginia and across the country, there are far fewer places where one can see the crucial decades of the emergence of contemporary America.

—DR. EDWARD L. AYERS
President and Professor of History
University of Richmond

known by his contemporaries, invested in rebuilding the Richmond and Danville Railroad and expanding it into the Deep South. Later he was a founder of the Seaboard Air Line Railway and served on the board of the Chesapeake and Ohio Railway.[8] Financed solely by Southern capital, the Seaboard joined many independent rail lines to form a direct connection from Richmond to Florida, which promised a new global prominence for the South. In a speech at its opening banquet in 1900, Major Dooley declared:

I announce to you gentlemen . . . the South is in the field for business. . . . Now that we have built our own furnaces, our own factories, mills, foundries, and our own railroads, where shall we look for consumers of our growing products and expanding industries? We must even look to the south and west, we must look to the great Pacific Ocean. . . . [The South] stands by Item One of the Jeffersonian Democracy—expansion, expansion in territory, expansion in business and expansion in power. . . . The other world powers are training for the race for business; let us not be laggards in the race.[9]

Major Dooley's involvement in railroads led to substantial investments in heavy industries, real estate, and other ventures. Touted by the *New York Star* in 1888 as one of "the prominent Southern men on Wall Street," he not only achieved his childhood dream of making a fortune, but at the same time he played an important role in the emergence of the New South.[10]

Sharing his wealth and influence to benefit his community, Major Dooley

Above: James Dooley poses with fellow members of the Courts of Justice Committee of the Virginia House of Delegates, circa 1871–73. He served three terms, and in 1877 he declined to run again for political office.

Right: The Richmond and Danville Railroad was among Major Dooley's early business ventures. One of its locomotives is shown here in the 1880s.

The Dooleys' summer home Swannanoa was designed by the prominent firm of Noland and Baskervill. It was completed in 1913 and is seen here circa 1915–25.

Below: At Swannanoa, the stained glass window designed by Tiffany Studios measures approximately twelve feet by twelve feet. It depicts a youthful Sallie Dooley in classical attire standing in an Italian garden.

served on the boards of St. Joseph's Orphan Asylum (now St. Joseph's Villa) in Richmond and the Medical College of Virginia (now the Virginia Commonwealth University Medical Center), to which he donated funds for a new hospital building. He also enjoyed leading the Art Club of Richmond as its president for an entire decade. As one of his associates remarked, Major Dooley "combined the art of making money with the love of art."[11] His affinity for European art is strongly evident in the character and contents of both Maymont and Swannanoa, the Dooleys' palatial Italian Renaissance-style summer home in Virginia's Blue Ridge Mountains.[12]

Sallie May was born on her grandparents' tobacco plantation in Lunenburg County, Virginia. She was steeped in the agrarian culture of the Old South. Her father, Dr. Henry May, was a physician from Petersburg. Her mother, Julia Jones, died when Sallie was only about seven years old. Later as an author, she expressed her nostalgia for the rural, antebellum world of her childhood. Her book, *Dem Good Ole Times*, published in 1906 by Doubleday, Page and Company, places her squarely in the literary tradition of Lost Cause apologists. Mrs. Dooley lavished particular attention on the gardens of Maymont and Swannanoa. She wrote, "I am so fond of such things that I always superintend the planting *myself*."[13] Descended from prominent, old Virginia families, she was the founding regent of the state's first chap-

Above right: Lady in the Garden was one of the watercolors painted by Suzanne Gutherz to illustrate Sallie Dooley's book, *Dem Good Ole Times*, published by Doubleday, Page and Co., 1906.

Above left: Sallie Dooley's Louis Vuitton steamer trunk, circa 1900.

ter of the Daughters of the American Revolution and was a charter member of the Society of Colonial Dames in the Commonwealth of Virginia. She also took a stand as a member of the Executive Committee of the Virginia Association Opposed to Woman's Suffrage. Although the couple had no children, they enjoyed the company of many nephews and nieces, including Nora Houston, an artist and suffragist, and Florence Elder, who lived with them for a time in the early twentieth century.

Major and Mrs. Dooley traveled widely throughout the United States, frequented fashionable resort areas, and enjoyed touring Europe. An article describing their 1910 sojourn abroad presents the very picture of luxurious travel in the Gilded Age. "They spent four or five weeks very delightfully among the hill towns of Italy . . . and are now in Paris, having traveled down the Rhine, and expect to remain in France for some time, motoring through the chateau country the later part of the month. They will also spend some time in England before returning to Richmond in the fall."[14] Though Southerners born and raised, they embraced a cosmopolitan outlook and thrived in the changing world around them.

While the Dooleys made many bequests to family members and to Maymont employees, they left the greatest portion of their wealth to Richmond charities. Major Dooley bequeathed $3 million to St. Joseph's orphanage, which at the time was said to have been the largest bequest ever made to a Catholic charity in the United States.[15] Upon his death in 1922, it was announced the couple had decided to give Maymont to the City of Richmond. When Mrs. Dooley died three years later, she left substantial bequests to the Richmond Public Library, the Children's Hospital, and the Virginia Diocese of the Protestant Episcopal Church.[16] Swannanoa was left to Major Dooley's surviving sisters. Along with the Maymont bequest, Mrs. Dooley gave a selection of nearly one thousand furnishings and works of art from their two residences to form the museum collection. Regrettably, all of the family papers in the mansion were destroyed shortly after Mrs. Dooley's death.[17] Opening to the public in 1926, Maymont immediately became a beloved Richmond oasis.

Portraits of James and Sallie Dooley by William Garl Brown, oil on canvas, 1889. These companion portraits were painted when plans for their new residence were being finalized.

THE MAYMONT MANSION

While taking a leisurely horseback ride west of Richmond, James and Sallie Dooley discovered farmland along the James River that they had never before visited. They were instantly captivated.

> Entering through Shield's Grove and coming down the hill, we came to this creek; then up the hill again until we got to this ridge, where we were greatly struck with the beauty of the views of the river and the beautiful oaks that were on the slope of that hill. . . . In 1886, I bought it from Dr. Crenshaw. We commenced to build the house in 1889, and in 1893 we finished it and went there to live.[18]

Formerly a dairy farm, the property totaled approximately one hundred acres of rolling terrain, a scenic setting for their grand estate. Combining Mrs. Dooley's maiden name of May with the French word for "hill," they named it Maymont.

To design their residence, the Dooleys engaged architect Edgerton Stewart Rogers (1860–1901), who was born and educated in Rome. With his mother being a Richmond native and his father the internationally known sculptor Randolph Rogers, the young man had little difficulty establishing his practice in Virginia. By the end of his brief career, Rogers had to his credit the country houses of two of

Above: This watercolor painted by Thomas Harrison Wilkinson in 1903 is one of the earliest images of the Maymont Mansion. Completed in 1893, the Dooleys' residence is shown with its original red slate roof.

Opposite: Blue Drawing Room.

THE MAYMONT MANSION · 21

The Moorish-style Den, a small anteroom near the south entrance.

the city's most prominent citizens and several public buildings. For the World's Columbian Exposition held in Chicago in 1893, he designed the Virginia Building, which he modeled after Mount Vernon. Of his works, only the Maymont Mansion remains.[19]

Rogers's design for the Dooleys reflects the widespread preference among architects in the late nineteenth century to draw inspiration from historical European styles. Designers also freely adapted styles from distant cultures of the world. When Maymont was conceived, the fashion for blending diverse traditions was at its peak in American taste. This trend was fueled by an explosion of knowledge and advanced by innovations in printing and photographic processes, which broadened the dissemination of information. Moreover, the increasing comfort and speed of travel exposed thousands of Americans to the cultural centers of Europe and beyond and to the great international expositions. With its castle-like turrets, Italian and Japanese gardens, and countless styles within the mansion, Maymont is a true embodiment of Gilded Age eclecticism.

Commanding pleasing vistas of the landscape and river, the highest point on the property was selected as the site for the residence. With broad sweeps of parkland spreading to its north and south, a long, magnolia-lined drive curves up a gentle slope to the mansion. At its end stands the Maymont Mansion, surrounded by expansive lawns with flowering trees, arching rose bowers, and towering exotic specimens. For the residence, Rogers combined Richardsonian Romanesque with French Château elements, including variously shaped towers and steeply pitched gables. The rough-cut stonework, bold round arches of the porte cochere, and the structure's overall rugged strength reflect the early medieval style adapted by American architect Henry Hobson Richardson. One distinctly American feature is the ample, curving porch with polished pink granite columns. Faced with buff-colored sandstone, the three-story, thirty-three-room structure is set on a full basement.[20] By 1893 the Dooleys' residence was complete.

Maymont is like a grand opera with a whole series of crescendos and dramatic highpoints—the Waterfall, for example, the Swan Room, the Tiffany Window, and the Italian Garden. It has one of the most intact American houses from the Gilded Age period. Maymont is extraordinary in that its contents and its landscape have survived so many years.

—DR. RICHARD GUY WILSON
Commonwealth Professor of Architectural History, University of Virginia and Host of *America's Castles*, A&E Network

Displaying the high-style taste of the late 1880s and 1890s, the mansion's interiors reveal the hand of a sophisticated but as yet unidentified designer. Preferences for European elegance and decorative complexity defined the desired look. Principal rooms were richly adorned with an array of patterns, tones, and textures juxtaposed with historical and international allusions. Contemporary tastemakers advised that each room have its own distinct theme, and Maymont interiors followed suit. A range of decorative elements was employed to this end, from stained glass, stenciling, and various ceiling and wall treatments to elaborately molded plasterwork, fine woodwork, parquet, and other costly embellishments. Spaces were filled with a multitude of *objets d'art*. The Maymont Mansion is a virtual encyclopedia of decorative arts of the period: French tapestries, oriental rugs, richly carved furniture, Neoclassical sculpture, fine European and Asian porcelain, Art Nouveau objects, and luxury items

The Library's rich detailing and wide array of furnishings demonstrate the fashionable décor of the Gilded Age. More than ninety-five percent of the collection displayed in the first- and second-floor rooms was owned by the Dooleys.

Below: This small cameo glass vase was made in the 1880s by Thomas Webb and Sons of England. Using multiple layers of colored glass, Webb's technique influenced later art glass makers.

Bottom: Silver deposit vase, engraved with Art Nouveau floral design and Sallie Dooley's monogram, circa 1900.

from Tiffany and Company. Decorative arts historian Kenneth L. Ames observes that a number of pieces are "quite unlike the objects the orthodox new rich elsewhere chose to collect. Maymont has some truly distinguished objects in its collections."[21]

Rare among historic house museums, the Maymont Mansion never underwent major alterations after the Dooleys' time. Although architectural drawings were among the papers destroyed following Mrs. Dooley's death, the fabric of the building and its extant contents have proved exceptional documents upon which to base the mansion's careful, three-decade-long restoration. As a result, the interiors today closely mirror their original appearance. Architectural historian Laurie Ossman places the Maymont Mansion "among the best examples of Gilded Age décor in America."[22]

Upstairs

Living Hall and Tiffany Stained Glass Window. Designed to make a dramatic first impression with the grand staircase rising three stories, the Living Hall was the centerpiece of the house plan. A massive, English Renaissance-inspired mantelpiece lends the character of a baronial hall to the space. Soaring fifteen feet above the hall, a stained glass window by Tiffany Glass and Decorating Company (later renamed Tiffany Studios) was placed with dazzling effect. The central panel of the lower tier depicts Christ standing in a doorway with "Peace Be Unto This House" inscribed on a banner. With swirling grapevines, the upper tier of the window is a brilliant expression of Art Nouveau. For a reception in February 1898, attended by four hundred guests and catered by Pompeo Maresi of New York City, the Living Hall was transformed into a virtual bower. "From bottom to top of the stairs was a fragrant network of ferns, smilax and pink roses, and a light was so placed as to bring out with vivid clearness the beauty of the large Tiffany stained glass window at the top of the stairs."[23]

Above: The lower tier of the fifteen-foot stained glass window by Tiffany Glass and Decorating Company, installed in 1892, is shown in detail.

Opposite: This large tapestry, circa 1787–94, made by the famous Gobelins Manufactory of France, represents *Don Quixote Freed of His Folly by Wisdom*. Dooley acquired it from Duveen, a leading international art dealer.

Above left: A bronze lion sculpted by Louis Amateis in 1891 guards the base of the grand staircase in the Living Hall.

Above right: The Living Hall mantelpiece decorated for Christmas.

Opposite top left: Jack-in-the-Pulpit vase, by Louis Comfort Tiffany, favrile glass, 20 in., 1908. An example of Tiffany's Art Nouveau design, the vase is a highly stylized expression of a woodland flower.

Opposite top center: Enamelware vase, 19½ in., circa 1900, by Kawaguchi Bunzaemon, a highly regarded Japanese cloisonné artist who won awards at several of the great international expositions.

Opposite top right: The Library mantelpiece.

Opposite bottom right: The carved figure of a winged lion—the emblem of St. Mark, patron saint of Venice—supports the back of this nineteenth-century chair inspired by Italian Renaissance motifs.

  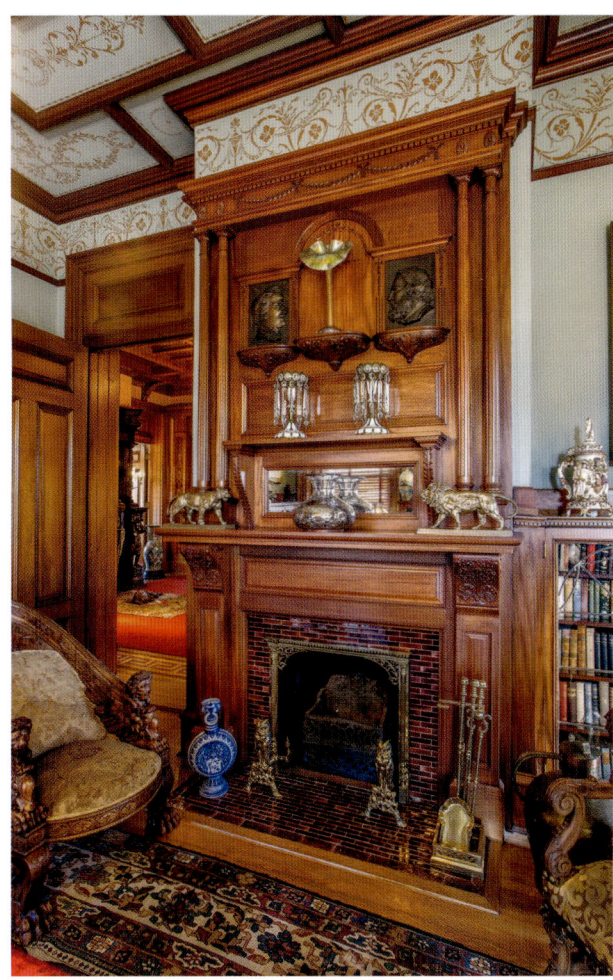

Library. Traditionally a masculine domain in the domestic sphere, the Library reveals Maymont as the home of a man of learning—a man who named among his most cherished distinctions the academic medals he won as a student at Georgetown and a man in whose memory the Richmond Public Library was built. Major Dooley received friends and business associates here and, in keeping with Victorian practice, retired to the Library with male guests for after-dinner brandy and cigars. Conveying the owner's broad appreciation of art, design, and culture, the room exemplifies the "artistic" taste of the day. Furnishings range from a Louis XV-style cylinder desk and an elaborately carved Italian Renaissance-style chair with winged lions to a lustrous Japanese enamelware vase by Kawaguchi and a Jack-in-the-Pulpit favrile glass vase by Louis Comfort Tiffany. Apropos the setting, the overmantel incorporates bronze portrait plaques of American poets Edgar Allan Poe and Henry Wadsworth Longfellow as well as Colonial Revival motifs.

Drawing Rooms. Maymont's adjoining drawing rooms demonstrate the sumptuous quality and French styling that was fashionable for formal reception areas of the era. Silk damask wall coverings, white onyx hearthstones, and ornate plasterwork amplify the suite's luxurious character. Architectural historian Richard Guy Wilson has called the Pink Draw-

ing Room a "high-calorie confection of Gilded Age design."[24] Depicting billowing clouds and lush blossoms, the delicately colored ceiling fresco captures the spirit of eighteenth-century Rococo art, thus establishing the Louis XV theme of the room. Embellished with a gilded mantel and gold-plated chandeliers, the room presented a splendid setting in which any grande dame of society would be proud to receive her guests. It was here that Mrs. Dooley greeted the throng at her 1898 reception. "Her gown was one of the works of art from the Worth establishment, with a front of cream-colored brocade embroidered in silver, corsage draped with exquisite lace, and a court train of green satin falling from just below the shoulders. Magnificent opals and diamonds and a large bouquet of lilies of the valley completed the costume."[25]

With its arched overmantel, decoratively painted doors, and French porcelain and tapestry-covered salon furniture, the Blue Drawing Room reflects the Louis XVI style. Aluminum leaf, then a costly and stylish novelty, highlights details of the woodwork, and silver-plated chandeliers and fitments further enrich the décor.

Opposite: Pink Drawing Room.

Above: The marble bust, circa 1880–93, in the Blue Drawing Room was sculpted by American artist William Couper. His large sculpture *Mother's Love*, circa 1880, is displayed in the Pink Drawing Room beyond.

Oyster Plate, Haviland and Company, porcelain, France, 1880.

Dining Room. A stately setting for formal, multi-course dinners, the Dining Room was the largest room in the house. The subdued tones of the painted wall coverings depicting garden scenes, along with the quarter-sawn oak wainscoting and coffered ceiling, provided a rich backdrop for the dazzling spectacle of the table setting. Befitting the high status of the social affairs enjoyed here, the Dining Room showcased treasures that were sure to capture the attention of the Dooleys' guests. Outstanding among these were the seventeenth-century sculpture *The Birth of Wine* by Italian artist Francesco Grassia, which Major Dooley purchased in Rome in 1910, and the monumental rosewood cabinet towering in its thirteen-foot niche. Designed by Jean-Paul Mazaroz, the cabinet was exhibited at the 1855 Exposition Universelle in Paris.[26] Filling this cabinet and others in the room is a limited-edition set of the flamboyant dinner service created by Haviland for the White House during the administration of President Rutherford B. Hayes. Today it is one of the largest public displays of this famous set.[27]

Above left: French ébéniste Jean-Paul Mazaroz created this Rococo Revival cabinet, measuring nearly thirteen feet tall, around 1850. Displayed inside are pieces from the Dooleys' duplicate set of the dinner service that Haviland and Company produced for the White House.

Above right: Theodore Davis painted 130 watercolors of American flora and fauna for the porcelain dinner service created by Haviland and Company in 1880. The fish platter depicts a shad caught in a golden net.

THE MAYMONT MANSION · 31

A Maymont Mansion place setting arranged for *service à la russe*, the preferred presentation style of formal dinners in the Gilded Age.

An article in 1904 describes the type of elegant entertaining that took place here. "Major Dooley is always a royal host and in his hospitality on this occasion he fairly excelled himself. The table was beautifully decorated in roses and maiden hair ferns, and the menu was delicious, many of the confections served being furnished by a prominent Washington caterer. The sparkle of wit vied with the wine, in which healths were drunk and good fellowship pledged."[28] Perhaps the most distinguished gathering at Maymont was the luncheon held for 250 guests in December 1912 for the National Governor's Conference in Richmond.[29]

Butler's Pantry. Located adjacent to the Dining Room, the Butler's Pantry was the domain of the highest ranking household employee. The butler's impeccable appearance and expert execution of proper service were important signs of the Dooleys' status. William Dilworth (1876–1961) held this position from 1919 to 1925. He answered the door, announced guests, supervised the presentation of meals, and attended the lady of the house when she served tea. Responsible for ensuring the upstairs spaces were orderly and clean, the butler supervised the housemaid and the assistant butler. The room was outfitted with a speaking tube, which allowed the butler and the cook in the basement kitchen to coordinate the arrival of food via the dumbwaiter. The Butler's Pantry also includes a copper-lined sink; cabinets for storing fine china, glassware, and silver; and a telephone for placing orders and answering calls for the Dooleys.

Trays and plates were prepared in the Butler's Pantry for service in the Dining Room.

Silver dragon-head finials ornament the four narwhal tusks of the Tiffany and Company dressing table and chair.

Swan Room. Mrs. Dooley's bedroom is one of Maymont's dramatic high points. With a decorative ceiling depicting a blue sky and flower garlands, the Swan Room is the dream-like setting of two of the mansion's greatest treasures. One is Mrs. Dooley's bed, designed in the shape of an enormous swan. The swan bed and its matching suite of furniture were acquired for her use at Swannanoa from Neuman and Company, the New York design firm that coordinated the interiors of the summer home. While artistic and mythological allusions to swans abound, the exact inspiration for the swan bed is not known. Nonetheless, this unique creation expresses the singular whim of a wealthy lady who delighted in fantasy and romance. Beside it stands a Tiffany and Company tour de force—the one-of-a-kind sterling-silver dressing table and chair designed in 1903. Setting it apart from all other silver showpieces of this era, the luxurious ensemble is fashioned from four entire narwhal tusks capped with dragon-head finials. The silverwork is elaborately chased with an intricate animal-interlace pattern and inlaid with narwhal tusk ivory. It is the ultimate expression of Tiffany's Viking style.[30]

Above: The Viking-style ensemble with dressing table, chair, and matching vanity set, created by Tiffany and Company between 1903 and 1905, was fashioned from sterling silver and narwhal tusks.

Opposite: Sallie Dooley's Bedroom is furnished with a swan bed and matching suite of painted and gilded wood, circa 1912.

THE MAYMONT MANSION · 35

Second Floor Living Hall and Other Rooms. Brilliantly lit by the Tiffany window, the spacious upper Living Hall was the room in which Mrs. Dooley, an avid bridge player, kept her card table ready for a game with friends. On special occasions when the orchestra from Richmond's Jefferson Hotel was engaged, musicians were seated in this area. A short hall to the left connected the Swan Room, a tiled bathroom, and the Cherry Bedroom, which Major Dooley probably occupied at first. In later years he used the East Bedroom Suite, which was likely planned as the principal guest room. The adjoining Morning Room decorated with maple woodwork served as an informal sitting room. Third-floor rooms at the top of the grand staircase were apparently intended for guests and various family purposes, including storage.[31]

Above: Portrait miniatures of James and Sallie Dooley and a copy of *Dem Good Ole Times* on a desk top in the Morning Room.

Above left: A detail of the upper tier of the stained glass window designed by Tiffany Glass and Decorating Company.

Household Technology

The Dooleys' home may have looked like a castle on the outside, but inside it was warm, bright, and outfitted with the latest conveniences. It was one of the first residences in the Richmond area to be equipped with electricity at the time of its construction. Since early electric lighting was not completely reliable, combination gas-electric fixtures, such as those in the Maymont Mansion, bridged the transition from gaslight. Gas was generated on the property by an air-gas machine. The Dooleys likely acquired their electricity through the city's streetcar system, the first successful electrified trolley system in the country. Electricity also powered the Otis elevator that was installed around 1910.

Water came from a spring north of Dooley Branch, a stream traversing the property. A hydraulic ram pumped water uphill to a holding tank in the tower of the adjacent outbuilding. This source supplied the household plumbing system, which included the bathrooms, kitchen, and various service rooms. Hot water was circulated through the house from a tall, cylindrical tank attached to the kitchen range. Fueled by a coal-burning furnace, the mansion's central indirect radiator system was then considered one of the most effective methods for heating large residences.

Below left: Combination gas-electric light fixtures were used throughout the mansion. All of the fixtures in the first- and second-floor rooms are original, including this gold-plated chandelier in the Pink Drawing Room.

Below right: Used to summon the domestic staff, the annunciator near the kitchen door was connected to call bells placed strategically in rooms on the first and second floors.

DOMESTIC WORKPLACE

In grand homes of the day, a large staff of skilled domestic employees was vital for maintaining the elegance and order of the household, preparing and serving meals, tending to the family's personal needs, and performing elaborate social rituals. From 1800 to 1920, the presence of domestic help in middle- and upper-class homes was common. The demand for household employees reached its zenith in the Gilded Age. A study conducted in 1897 revealed that Richmond and Washington, D.C., tied for the highest domestic employment rate among all major American cities. In other regions of the country, the domestic labor force was largely drawn from new immigrant populations. At the time when the Maymont Mansion was built—only twenty-eight years after the end of the Civil War—old patterns continued in the South, with African Americans filling most domestic jobs. Enforcing racial segregation and limiting civil rights, strict Jim Crow laws were enacted during the May-

The domestic staff of a prominent Richmond household, circa 1905.

mont era. Such laws compounded the hardships of low income, poor housing, and limited options for education and employment for African Americans.[32]

The Maymont domestic staff—nearly all African Americans—generally numbered from seven to ten employees who filled the positions of butler, assistant butler, cook, kitchen maid, housemaid, lady's maid, and laundress. They typically worked a thirteen-hour day and were given one to two afternoons off each week. Their wages were comparable to, and in some cases higher than, those of workers in other upper-class Richmond households.[33]

Maymont and other well-to-do homes of the era were designed to limit intersection of the worlds of server and served. One Victorian housekeeping manual represents the distinctly *upstairs* perspective. "The housekeeping . . . should move like perfect, well-oiled machinery, with invisible wheels. Let the comforts and luxuries provided for your family and guests come to them as by magic."[34] The "household machine," however, was comprised of individuals who had few options to get ahead in life. The granddaughter of head butler William Dilworth expressed the *downstairs* counterpoint. "My grandfather went to work to do a job, but to do it invisibly. . . . 'Get the job done, come and serve me, but be quiet about it.' But at home he was our 'Papa.' He was not invisible to us. He was the heart of our family, our moral compass."[35]

Head butler William Dilworth and his wife Mary in 1956. Major Dooley insisted that everyone refer to him as "Mr. Dilworth." He and other domestic employees were remembered by Sallie Dooley in her will.

The mansion's service spaces included a separate entrance for staff and deliverymen, the Butler's Pantry, the narrow backstairs, and the principal utilitarian zone in the basement. Full-size windows in most rooms and high ceilings give a spacious feel to the belowstairs rooms: the Kitchen, Kitchen Pantry, Cold Pantry, Wine Cellar, Laundry Room, Maids' Bedroom, and Butler's Bedroom in addition to the furnace and coal storage rooms. The restored spaces, now filled with furnishings and household accessories of the period, provide insight into the lives of domestic employees, their important role in operating a great Southern household, and the challenges they faced beyond the workplace during the Jim Crow era.

Downstairs

Kitchen. The Kitchen was the hub of downstairs activity. Here, the head cook prepared meals on the double-oven, coal-fired range. Frances Twiggs Walker (1864–1928) filled this important position from 1919 to 1925. She was skilled in all types of fare, including fine cuisine, teatime specialties, such as nasturtium sandwiches, and regional favorites, such as beaten biscuits. Three of her daughters served sequentially as the kitchen maid, who was responsible for assisting the cook with preparing meals and cleaning. The Kitchen also functioned as a dining area for the household staff, where, according to descendants, they were entertained by a talking parrot.

Mrs. Walker's niece, Virgie Payne, recalled the memorable day when she was introduced to Mrs. Dooley, who remarked, "I hope that you will grow up to become a fine cook like your aunt." Her aunt responded emphatically, "Thank you, ma'am, but I don't want her to be a cook," perhaps implying her hope that the younger generation would have opportunities that she and others lacked.[36]

Many descendants of the domestic staff shared recollections that helped to give authenticity to the restoration of the Kitchen and other belowstairs rooms.

Maids' Room. By day, this large, bright, and well-ventilated space served as a workroom for mending and ironing. Flatirons were heated on the laundry stove located in this room. Housemaids' tasks ranged from dusting, sweeping, and polishing to beating carpets, washing windows, scrubbing bathrooms, and changing sheets. The lady's maid was responsible for all matters related to Mrs. Dooley's wardrobe and grooming. By night, two or three young women on the household staff slept here. While some domestics returned to their own lodgings at night, those who "lived in," even after retiring to bed, might be summoned upstairs at any time by the ring of a bell.

Above: Maids' Room.

Left: Frances Walker (1904–1981), employed at Maymont as a kitchen maid, was the daughter of head cook Frances Twiggs Walker. Years later, her daughter, Doris Walker Woodson, served on the Maymont Foundation Board of Directors, 2003–09.

Head butler William Dilworth cherished the illustration (*right*) that now hangs in the Butler's Bedroom. His grandson, Harold P. Bailey, donated it to Maymont.

Butler's Bedroom. This quiet corner room was the sleeping quarters for one of the two men on the household staff. When William Dilworth was head butler, he maintained his own home and returned to his family each night, leaving this room available to Justin Sims, the assistant butler. According to family stories, even when the Dooleys' dined alone, both the butler and assistant butler, dressed in formal attire, stood in attendance at either end of the table. The assistant butler may also have functioned as Major Dooley's valet.

The image now displayed in this bedroom, titled "Jesus Died for Both," hung in the Dilworth home.

42 · MAYMONT: AN AMERICAN ESTATE

Above: The Kitchen Pantry shelves are stocked with canned and packaged foods.

Above left: Major Dooley likely stockpiled his favorite wines and liquors in the Wine Cellar before Prohibition was enacted in Virginia in 1916, four years prior to the constitutional amendment. Only he and the butler had keys to this room.

The laundress used this triple sink unit in the Laundry Room for soaking, scrubbing, and rinsing. Spending long hours lifting hot kettles and heavy irons, she laundered everything from delicate lace shirtwaists to enormous damask tablecloths.

The Cold Pantry where fish, meat, cheese, fruit, and other perishables were stored.

DOMESTIC WORKPLACE · 43

ESTATE LANDSCAPE AND GARDENS

Mrs. Dooley has devoted her time and energies and her studies to making this place beautiful. Altogether we have made the place an ornament and a credit to the city of Richmond.

—JAMES H. DOOLEY, 1906 [37]

An artfully designed landscape and architectural complex surrounding the grand residence was an essential element of the Gilded Age estate. Created at considerable cost and requiring meticulous ongoing care by a small army of workers—twenty were employed at Maymont—a high-maintenance landscape was perhaps the ultimate sign of affluence. While enhancing the natural beauty of the site, developing the grounds also offered further opportunities for the owners to express their personal tastes and interests. At Maymont, the Dooleys extended the stylish eclecticism of the mansion into the landscape through the addition of thematic gardens and estate buildings inspired by historical European styles.

Maymont's one-hundred-acre historic landscape and architectural complex are remarkably intact. The James River defines the southern boundary of the estate.

Opposite: Peonies billow around the base of the Venetian Gazebo that Major Dooley called "our beautiful temple."

The Italianate Gazebo with red slate roof is one of several original summer houses that ornament the landscape.

Three granite quarries existed on the property prior to the Dooleys' ownership. This one, shown in a 1903 watercolor by Thomas Harrison Wilkinson, is today the Black Bear Habitat.

Characteristic of Virginia's fall-line terrain, the site—with its high bluffs, granite outcroppings, broad uplands, deep ravines, and streams—provided an excellent canvas for creating a landscape of great drama.[38] The Dooleys' vision evolved over the years. Establishing the lawns, as Major Dooley explained, was one of the first challenges. English-style parkland bound the complex together and provided naturalistic vistas and a scenic backdrop for the architecture. During the first decade drives, walkways, outbuildings, specimen trees, statuary, abundant floral displays, and gazeboes in various styles were added to the grounds. Describing their early efforts, Major Dooley recalled that they "put out six hundred rose bushes and

thousands of flowers, and purchased the most costly evergreens and all of those beautiful cherry trees they have in Japan, at great cost."³⁹

One spring Mrs. Dooley sent a bouquet of roses to the *Richmond Dispatch*, which printed a note of gratitude for all to see. "Mrs. Dooley is devotedly fond of her flowers, and the rare perfection of these are in no small degree due to her thought and labor upon their growth."⁴⁰ A sunset "at home" in June 1900 offers a glimpse of the Dooleys enjoying the grounds with their friends. "Mrs. Dooley received her guests on the lawn, which, with its velvety sward and splendid trees, looked never more beautiful."⁴¹ She walked the grounds daily with the trusted, long-term estate manager, Louis Walker Taliaferro (1875–1943).⁴²

In the early twentieth century, the Dooleys embarked on a second building campaign that was even more ambitious than the first. They engaged Noland and Baskervill, a prominent Richmond firm, to add new formal gardens, fountains, substantial outbuildings, and other refinements. Architects William Churchill Noland (1865–1951) and Henry Eugene Baskervill (1867–1946) contributed many notable structures to the Richmond skyline during their partnership. They also designed Swannanoa, the Dooleys' lavish summer home, which was completed in 1913.⁴³ Major Dooley sent Baskervill to Italy to select marble for Swannanoa's interior and garden ornaments as well as to gather inspiration for both of the Dooley estates.⁴⁴ By 1912 the couple's vision for Maymont had been largely realized. Indeed, it became the unrivaled Richmond showplace of its day.

Above left: The Three Graces is based on a famous work by the nineteenth-century Italian sculptor Antonio Canova.

Below: The Italian Garden pergola, shown in a 1939 photograph, is today the romantic setting of many weddings.

ESTATE LANDSCAPE AND GARDENS · 47

ARBORETUM

Maymont's collection of trees is recognized as one of the country's distinguished, century-old arboreta, with thousands of trees and shrubs representing more than three hundred different species from around the world. In the nineteenth century, plant exploration and the enthusiasm for creating ornamental estates led to a great wave of importation of exotic species and the development of many new cultivars. The Dooleys embraced this trend with a passion, establishing a planting program of considerable magnitude. Many trees that were planted during their time still survive. Their size and age indicate careful placement and planting that allowed for optimum long-term growth. Noteworthy imported specimens include the Persian Ironwood (*Parrotia persica*); False Golden Larch (*Pseudolarix amabilis*) and Weeping Scholar Tree (*Sophora japonica "Pendula"*), both from China; Blue Atlas Cedar (*Cedrus atlantica "Glauca"*) from North Africa; Nordman Fir (*Abies nordmanniana*) from the Caucasus; Spanish Fir (*Abies pinsapo*); and a number of fine Deodar Cedars (*Cedrus deodora*), a species from Afghanistan and Nepal. Among Maymont's revered old American natives are the Southern Magnolia (*Magnolia grandiflora*) and a champion Darlington Oak (*Quercus hemisphaerica*). Today the majestic trees of the estate lend a special grandeur to Maymont that is rarely found at public places in the United States.

Above left: Ginkgo, near the Dooley Mausoleum.

Above right: Blue Atlas Cedar, northwest of the Maymont Mansion.

Below: Persian Ironwood near the Italian Garden.

Opposite: Deodar Cedars south of the Stone Barn.

ITALIAN GARDEN

One of the most popular additions to Gilded Age estates was an Italian garden. The Dooleys' choice of this style reflects their strong affinity for Italy, which is echoed in the style of their summer home and in the artwork they collected. Designed by Noland and Baskervill, the garden was completed in 1910. According to a contemporary account, the architects used "drawings, photographs and measurements of the best specimens of this character of artistic work abroad" and promised "under Virginia skies, on the hills above the falls of the James, the same effects as in the palatial estates of Southern Europe."[45]

The Dooleys' garden embodies many traditional elements of the style, which has evolved since the Renaissance. It is arrayed in balustraded terraces on a south-facing hillside overlooking the James River. A stone arch with the Latin inscription *Via Florum* marks the formal entrance to the garden. Offering dappled shade, a long rose-covered pergola, supported by rusticated granite columns and terminated by a dome, forms the axis of the upper terrace, with geometrically patterned flower beds, fountains, and classical urns. The focal point of the vista to the east is a gazebo that Major Dooley acquired in Venice.[46] From the lower terrace, the Cascade descends the hillside. Its design is based on a feature of the Villa Torlonia at Frascati near Rome.[47] Adjacent to the Cascade, a naturalistic waterfall—the most spectacular man-made element of the landscape—plunges forty-five feet over a massive outcropping.

Outstanding features of the Italian Garden include the Cascade (*above*), the flower-filled parterres of the upper terrace, and the pergola (*opposite*). In summer *Rosa* 'Ginger' and *R.* 'Spartan' provide a colorful border.

Right: On a hillside above the James River, the Dooleys created an elegant garden similar to ones they had visited in Italy.

The Italian Garden was designed by Noland and Baskervill and completed in 1910. A granite arch with the inscription *Via Florum* marks the formal entrance to the garden. Climbing roses have been restored along the pergola.

Above: Lady Banks roses, *Rosa banksiae* 'Lutea,' grow in profusion along a lower terrace.

GROTTO

Enhancing the eclecticism of the landscape, the Dooleys added a Grotto in the steep hillside below the Italian Garden. Originating in ancient Rome, grottoes were traditionally intended as places to contemplate the irregular and hidden aspects of nature. Maymont's Grotto is a rare American example of this type of landscape feature. Its opening is studded with stalactites and stalagmites collected from caves in the Virginia mountains. Water channeled from a spring trickles down the walls encrusted with cave formations. The pebble-mosaic forecourt displays the heraldic symbol of Florence and is flanked by copies of lion sculptures by the Italian artist Antonio Canova.

JAPANESE GARDEN

In keeping with the fascination with Japan that swept Europe and the United States at the turn of the twentieth century, the Dooleys engaged a Japanese garden master to design a special landscape feature in his native style. Maymont's Japanese Garden is attributed to Y. Muto, who also developed gardens in Philadelphia at Compton (now the Morris Arboretum) and at Fairmount Park, as well as at estates in Tuxedo Park and on Long Island in New York.[48] Completed in 1912, the Dooleys' Japanese Garden is situated at the base of an old quarry on the property, with the Waterfall providing a spectacular backdrop. A sparkling stream lined with stones and native Japanese plantings meanders through the garden. The original garden also featured an earthen bridge and two small pavilions, one with fan-shaped windows and another perched on a ledge of the Waterfall. A handsome Katsuga-

Above: The moss-covered Hill Garden lies beyond the Moon Bridge.

Opposite: The Waterfall created during the Dooleys' time plunges forty-five feet over a massive granite outcropping.

JAPANESE GARDEN · 55

Shaded by a grove of Bald Cypress trees, the Japanese Garden pond presents a scene of placid beauty with colorful koi and stepping stones leading to an island.

style lantern, a smaller stone lantern, and original plantings date to the Dooleys' time. Art historian Kendall H. Brown notes Muto's trademark—"his dramatic use of stones"—plays a prominent role in his design at Maymont.[49]

After Mrs. Dooley's death, the Japanese Garden gradually deteriorated. In 1978 Maymont Foundation engaged Barry Starke of Earth Design, Inc., to plan its renovation. While preserving the core of Muto's garden, the plan added many new elements and enlarged the size of the garden. Now representing a Japanese stroll garden, it is composed of a system of paths that offer changing impressions of nature as different areas come into view. Much like those in Japan, the garden employs various features to convey a contemplative mood and to evoke an old, naturally developed landscape. From handcrafted Entrance Gates, the pathway leads past a Dry Pool—a place to stop and meditate upon sand patterns and rocks—and the enchanting, moss-covered Hill Garden, a "landscape in miniature" with a narrow winding watercourse. The two streams of the garden flow into a large pond, which was not part of the original Japanese Garden but rather a water garden that the Dooleys created from a turning basin of the old Kanawha Canal.[50] An *azumaya*, or small rustic pavilion, now overlooks the pond, which is filled with colorful koi (Japanese carp). In the Japanese manner, groupings of stones are carefully arranged throughout the garden, and a variety of bridges—Moon Bridge, Plank Bridge, Earthen Bridge, and Stepping Stones—encourages visitors to slow their pace and enjoy the beautiful surroundings.

Above: The Katsuga-style stone lantern dates to the original 1912 garden.

Below: An *azumaya* overlooks the Japanese Garden pond.

ESTATE BUILDINGS

The outbuildings of Gilded Age country houses not only served the practical needs of the estate, but they also contributed to the visual appeal of the complex. From the perspective of guests arriving at Maymont, the towers, gables, and varied rooflines of the outbuildings presented a picturesque panorama with a decidedly "Old World" character. This village-like assemblage, situated along the service road, was the central work zone that supported the operation and maintenance of the property and the Dooleys' lifestyle. During a typical day, the area would have been teeming with groundskeepers and gardeners, stable hands and coachmen, domestic workers coming and going to the mansion, deliverymen, and later, the Dooleys' chauffeur. Though Maymont was not a farm, a few cows and chickens were kept to supply fresh milk and eggs for the household, in addition to carriage horses, saddle horses, and draft horses required for mowing and hauling.

Maymont's estate outbuildings create a picturesque panorama lining the service road, which intersects with Magnolia Drive. The James River flows along Maymont's southern boundary.

58 · MAYMONT: AN AMERICAN ESTATE

The granite and gray brick barn was designed by Noland and Baskervill in 1908. Horse stalls were on the main level, with a hayloft above and cow stalls on the lower level. The barn served as the Nature Center from 1952 to 1999. The Herb Garden in the foreground was added in 1957 and is cared for by the Old Dominion Herb Society.

Outbuildings constructed during the estate's first decade included the modest Gatehouse, the residence of the estate manager; the Coop; and a three-story stable that was later renovated as the Dooleys' Garage. In the early twentieth century, Noland and Baskervill transformed the complex with the addition of several prominent structures, including the Carriage House, Stone Barn, Water Tower, Compost House (now the Garden Hall), Fountain Court, and two pump houses.

Garage

Edgerton Rogers, architect of the mansion, probably designed the frame-and-brick outbuilding that the Dooleys adapted as their garage around 1920. Initially it may have served as the main staging area for planting and maintaining the extensive ornamental landscape. The distinctive octagonal tower housed a large holding tank for the estate's drinking water.[51] On the third story, several finished rooms were occupied by estate employees.[52]

The Dooleys were among the first Richmonders to own automobiles. These included a Winton limousine (acquired around 1914), a 1918 Pierce Arrow, a 1919 Packard seven-passenger Landaulet, and other motorcars. Chauffeur James R. L. Fitzgerald (1892–1967) recalled that as soon as they left the gates of Maymont, Major Dooley always instructed him to drive "as fast as the law permits."[53]

Above: The Dooleys' Winton limousine with chauffeur James Fitzgerald at the wheel in 1916.

Left: The Dooleys employed James Fitzgerald as their chauffeur from 1914 to 1917.

ESTATE BUILDINGS · 59

Carriage House

Designed by Noland and Baskervill in 1904, the Normandy-style Carriage House is faced with granite that was likely quarried on the property. Horse stalls and  two projecting carriage bays open onto an inner courtyard where horses were harnessed and put to the carriages. The harness room was conveniently located nearby. On the second floor were the hayloft, grain storage, and coachman's quarters.

In the Gilded Age, fine carriages and horses became symbols of status and carriage driving a pastime of the affluent. A longtime member of the Deep Run Hunt Club, Major Dooley loved horses—in fact, the crest of the Dooley coat of arms is a horse's head (*left*). In their younger years, he and his wife enjoyed horseback riding, and at Maymont they frequently took carriage drives around the grounds. Equestrian and driving events were an enjoyable part of their social scene. After a deep snow in the winter of 1886, Major Dooley, driving a double cutter pulled by two black horses, joined in the fun of a sleighing event on the streets of Richmond. According to the newspaper account, "The merry sleighers flew along to the music of bells from one end of the fashionable thoroughfare to the other." Decades later one of his trotting horses, Jeff Davis, was awarded two first prizes, and two of his carriage horses, Tenant and Fairfax, won a first prize for "The Best Pair of Matched Horses Shown to a Suitable Vehicle." In 1900 Mrs. Dooley rode in a beautifully decorated carriage at Richmond's Floral Carriage Parade, a festival staged to celebrate the turn of the century.[54]

Today, the Carriage House displays horse-drawn vehicles appropriate for an estate inventory: formal coachman-driven carriages, such as the elegant Victoria by Brewster and Company, the preeminent American maker of carriages (*see right*); sporting vehicles, such as the Roof Seat Break for countryside outings; and pleasure carriages, such as the Lady's Basket Phaeton. A Thalhimer's Department Store delivery wagon (circa 1900) and a hearse represent distinct types of commercial vehicles of the period.

Left: Nieces and nephews of Sallie Dooley riding atop a Roof Seat Break on an outing near Staunton, Virginia, in 1897.

Opposite top: The Carriage House and Water Tower.

ESTATE BUILDINGS · 61

Water Tower and Fountain Court

Noland and Baskervill designed the immense Normandy-style Water Tower in 1908 both to add drama to the architectural complex and to perform the critical function of supplying water to the landscape's elaborate features. A gasoline-powered pump brought water from the Kanawha Canal into the tower. Assisted by gravity, water flowed from the tower to Fountain Court and on to the Italian Garden fountains, the Cascade, and the Waterfall. Fountain Court was designed by Noland and Baskervill in 1911. Originally nine feet deep, this elegant balustraded pool evidently served, like its Italian model at the Villa Torlonia, as a reservoir to feed the water features in the gardens below.[55]

Water from Fountain Court originally fed the fountains in the gardens below.

Mausoleum

The final addition to the grounds during the Dooley era was the Doric-style Mausoleum designed by Henry E. Baskervill and his new partner, Garey Lambert. Described by architectural historian Calder Loth as "a demure architectural jewel," the Mausoleum was inspired by two elegant monuments of ancient Greek architecture.[56] Completed in 1923, it provides a suitably dignified resting place for Major and Mrs. Dooley in the midst of their beloved estate.

The Dooley Mausoleum, located on a hillside near the mansion, overlooks the James River.

FROM PRIVATE RESIDENCE TO PUBLIC MUSEUM AND PARK

In accordance with her husband's will, Sallie Dooley left Maymont to the City of Richmond to be used as a museum and park. Even though they made several significant bequests to Richmond charities, the couple chose not to leave an endowment for the maintenance of Maymont. In March 1926, six months after Mrs. Dooley's death, Maymont opened to the public. The response was overwhelming. Virginia's travel magazines and newspapers rhapsodized on the beauties of the grounds and gardens. Visiting Maymont soon became established as a Richmond tradition.

Following World War II, civic leader William B. Thalhimer Sr. and a group of like-minded friends proposed the development of outdoor animal exhibits at Maymont. The first series of exhibits was completed in 1959 along Dooley Branch and in parkland north of the ravine that divides the property. Complementing the wildlife exhibits, the Richmond Council of Garden Clubs opened Maymont's first nature center in the Stone Barn in 1952. The group also created the Herb Garden four years later.

Despite local affection for Maymont, the estate fell into a period of deterioration that persisted for more than four decades. Garden statuary was vandalized, stonework began to crumble, and the precious arboretum was neglected. The mansion went unheated, its exterior woodwork remained unpainted, and persistent leaks damaged delicate interior detailing and furnishings. The glittering interiors and beautiful gardens that visitors enjoy today stand in stark contrast to their dire condition in 1970, when a *Richmond Times-Dispatch* article, "Dooley Museum is City's Albatross," reported a preservation nightmare.[57] The resulting public outcry led to the beginning of the rehabilitation of the mansion and the grounds.

Opposite: In June 1958, William B. Thalhimer Sr. broke ground near Dooley Branch for Maymont's first outdoor wildlife exhibits, with family, friends, and city officials in attendance.

Above: A vintage postcard, circa 1940.

Left: Visitors flocked to Maymont after it was opened to the public in 1926.

Right: Easter Sunday, 1966.

Below: Young ladies in 1928 pause near Dooley Branch.

While urgent repairs progressed, the need for continuing rehabilitation, ongoing care, and thoughtful development of Maymont's resources became obvious. In response, the City of Richmond entrusted the estate to the nonprofit Maymont Foundation, formerly the Thalhimer-Virginia Wildlife Foundation. In 1975 the foundation assumed responsibility for the estate's operation and maintenance and for development of its rich potential. In its first decade, Maymont Foundation addressed many pressing capital needs and launched educational programs, special events, and a still-thriving volunteer program. The Nature Center was renovated, and new wildlife habitats and a new Children's Farm were built. Elisabeth Scott Bocock, daughter of Frederic W. Scott, a business associate of Major Dooley, established the Carriage Collection. Restoration of the Italian Garden began through one of the first grants awarded for an historic landscape by the Heritage Conservation and Recreation

 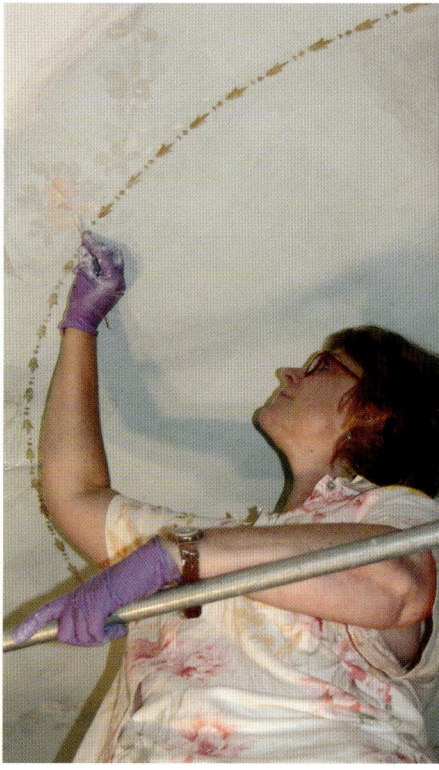

Service of the United States Department of the Interior. Rejuvenation of the Japanese Garden also began with the assistance of Ikebana of Richmond, and Maymont's fountains and Waterfall flowed once more.

After long years of neglect and abuse, the transformation of the Maymont Mansion into a professionally managed historic house museum commenced around 1980. Conservation of collections and a careful, comprehensive restoration ensued, a long-term endeavor that has been supported by the Maymont Council, founded in 1983 by civic leader and preservationist Mary Tyler Cheek McClenahan, and by many federal and private grants. Continuing commitment to Maymont's preservation ensures that one of the nation's outstanding Gilded Age estates will survive as an important historic and cultural resource for generations to come.

DALE CYRUS WHEARY
Curator/Director, Historial Collections and Programs
Maymont Foundation

Left: Maymont Foundation staff member Fred Murray accepted bear cubs for the Wildlife Exhibits in 1980.

Right: Conserving Maymont is an ongoing process. The ceiling painting in the Swan Room was meticulously restored in 2006.

Maymont Today

The Dooleys' estate, once enjoyed by invitation only, is now open to the public year-round and enjoyed annually by more than 500,000 guests from all walks of life and all parts of the world. With a range of experiences appealing to diverse interests and all ages, Maymont is naturally one of Richmond's favorite places. Guests are free to explore the estate, whether they wish to stroll through the gardens, observe wildlife, feed a friendly farm animal, tour the mansion and carriage display, or just sit under a lovely tree on a quiet hillside. It is truly a place for all seasons: spring brings masses of tulips and baby animals to the farm; summertime offers concerts on the lawn and cool, shady streams; in fall, brilliant color infuses the landscape; and in winter, the mansion is splendidly decorated for a Victorian Christmas. Maymont is a wonderful place to learn about the past, about horticulture, and about nature. In-depth experiences, school programs, group visits, carriage rides, special events, living history, summer camps, and private celebrations are held throughout the year. It is not surprising that the vast majority of visitors come back again and again.

A century after the Dooleys lived at Maymont, the estate remains a vital part of life in Richmond, offering a delightful setting for large public events, romantic weddings and limitless exploration.

Families enjoy strolling the grounds and gardens.

Costumed interpreters and horse-drawn carriages bring the Gilded Age to life for special programs and events at Maymont.

HISTORIC MANSION, GARDENS, AND OUTBUILDINGS

When guests step through the wrought-iron gates of Maymont, they enter a world of timeless elegance and natural beauty. Walking amid gabled outbuildings and inviting lawns, lingering in the Herb Garden, feeling the spray of the soaring fountain, and seeing horse-drawn carriages along Magnolia Drive, guests feel transported to another realm.

Down a winding path lined with stately trees, guests discover the romantic, flower-filled Italian Garden, where fountains play and roses trail on the elegant pergola. This fairytale sight is the setting for numerous weddings throughout the year. Granite stairs along the Cascade lead to the serenity of the Japanese Garden, where the Waterfall and Moon Bridge present one of Maymont's most memorable views. Resting in the *azumaya*, visitors enjoy watching colorful koi fish and children crossing the pond on the stepping stones.

At the heart of the estate, the towers of the Maymont Mansion vie with the treetops of magnificent evergreens planted over one hundred years ago. Touring the twenty-one restored rooms, guests learn the fascinating story of the Dooleys, how their estate was created, and what life was like in the Gilded Age. Guests often compare the opulent interiors to a jewel box. Belowstairs rooms appear as if work might resume at any moment. Upstairs and downstairs, the Maymont Mansion conveys a very tangible sense of a time gone by.

Christmas Tree in the Blue Drawing Room.

WILDLIFE EXHIBITS

Native wildlife species, some undoubtedly seen crossing the Dooleys' manicured lawns or soaring overhead a century ago, can be found in naturalistic outdoor habitats along the valley of Dooley Branch. The Wildlife Exhibits, first introduced in the late 1950s, are a sanctuary for animals that are injured, orphaned, or otherwise unable to survive in the wild. White-tailed deer gather on a shady knoll alongside American bison, the largest land mammals in North America. Although bison no longer live in the Virginia wilderness, they roamed the region through the eighteenth century. Guests can also see sika deer, a species introduced from Asia to the Eastern Shore of Virginia in the 1920s. In one of the old quarries on the property, black bears climb trees, swim in a pond, frolic, and dig within their sprawling habitat. Families make a game of spotting their camouflaged, sleeping forms among the rock outcroppings on lazy afternoons. Across a bridge, guests encounter majestic birds of prey, including bald eagles, hawks, owls, and vultures nestled among the trees in Raptor Valley. Meandering pathways lead to habitats of two of the Commonwealth's most elusive nocturnal predators, the grey fox and the bobcat.

Bobcats, bears, bison, and eagles are among the species protected in the Wildlife Exhibits at Maymont. Children learn about the wingspans of birds of prey in Raptor Valley.

CHILDREN'S FARM

Friendly farm animals are the big draw at the Children's Farm, a popular destination for young families and the first memory of Maymont for many guests. Maymont was not a farm in the Dooleys' time, but this well-loved corner of the estate is now a hub of activity and home to goats, sheep, chickens, domestic rabbits, donkeys, cows, pigs, and horses. An unusual sight in the middle of a capital city, the area offers hands-on animal encounters and insight into daily farm life that many urban and suburban guests otherwise may not experience. Children and adults alike are delighted by the crow of a rooster, the feel of a sheep's wool, and the nudge of a goat. Each visit to the farm is different, depending on the hour and the season, from bouncing baby goats in the spring to the "animal parade" at the end of each day. Surrounding the barn and pastures, open spaces are perfect for picnics and play time, while Marie's Butterfly Trail, Jack's Vegetable Garden, and a daylily and daffodil garden paint the landscape with rainbows of color.

Young guests enjoy interacting with goats, roosters, sheep, and other domesticated animals at the Children's Farm.

THE ROBINS NATURE CENTER

Along the southern edge of Maymont, the historic James River flows through the heart of Richmond on its journey from the Appalachian Mountains to the Chesapeake Bay. It was a beautiful sight that the Dooleys admired from the hilltop of their home. Today, its wildlife and wonders are the centerpiece of The Robins Nature Center on Maymont's northern boundary. Like a window into the river itself, a series of giant aquariums holds native animal species, including a variety of freshwater fish and turtles as well as playful river otters. Guests also see animals from habitats along the river's edge, such as snakes, frogs, and lizards. Interactive exhibits engage the senses with hands-on learning about the power and uses of the river. Guests can view a detailed topographical map of the hundred-acre estate, learn about programs and activities, and find souvenirs and snacks. The Robins Nature Center is the focal point of environmental education at Maymont, where educators present public programs and school field trips for thousands of children each year to foster respect for animals and to promote conservation of the natural world.

At the Nature Center visitors of all ages can see river otters as well as a variety of reptiles and fish.

AN EXTRAORDINARY GIFT

Something wonderful greets guests each day when they arrive at Maymont. It might be the sounds of splashing fountains and children at play. Or the twinkle of frost on massive evergreens. It might be a beam of sunlight striking the Tiffany window. Or the anticipation of a new baby goat at the farm. Each remarkable moment is a small part of the extraordinary gift, given to the community and the world, by James and Sallie Dooley. Their spirit of generosity has allowed generations to enjoy Maymont's wonders, and it has been an inspiration to others to preserve and enhance the one-hundred-acre estate. Countless donations have made possible historical restoration, renovations, and new additions, while volunteers have given thousands of hours year after year to host tours, plant gardens and much more. The Dooleys' legacy has inspired a circle of giving to preserve a Richmond treasure that, in turn, enriches the lives of its guests with priceless experiences and breathtaking beauty. Maymont today is an enchanting place that connects us to history, nature, and each other, and with continuing care, its timeless grace and inspiration will flourish for years to come.

Italian Garden at sunset.

NOTES

1. Etta Donnan Mann, *Four Years in the Governor's Mansion of Virginia, 1910–1914* (Richmond: Dietz Press, 1937), 151.

2. Information in the text is largely drawn from the Maymont Mansion Archives and curatorial research files. The author wishes to thank the many volunteers, staff, interns, and other colleagues who have contributed to these resources.

3. "American Millionaires," *New York Tribune Monthly*, vol. 4 (June 1892), 55.

4. Inscribed in *An Abridgement of Ainsworth's Dictionary of English and Latin*, ed. Thomas Morell (Philadelphia: n.d.). Maymont Mansion Collection.

5. John Edward Dooley, *John Dooley's Civil War: An Irish American's Journey in the First Virginia Infantry Regiment*, ed. Robert Emmett Curran (Knoxville: University of Tennessee Press, 2012).

6. R. A. Brock, *Virginia and Virginians* (Richmond and Toledo: H. H. Hardesty, 1888), 778–79. See also Lyon G. Tyler, *Men of Mark in Virginia*, vol. 1 (Washington, D.C.: Men of Mark Publishing, 1906), 167–68.

7. Maymont Mansion Archives.

8. Brock, *Virginia and Virginians*, and Tyler, *Men of Mark*.

9. James H. Dooley, "Our Foreign Commerce and the Open Doors," Seaboard Air Line Railway Opening Banquet, June 2, 1900. Quoted by Mary Lynn Bayliss, *Will the Real Major Dooley Please Stand Up and other Maymont Moments* (private printing, 2005), 57–59.

10. Mary Lynn Bayliss, "Major Dooley and the Richmond and Danville Railroad," *Maymont Notes*, no. 3 (2003–04), 17.

11. William A. MacCorkle, *The Recollections of Fifty Years of West Virginia* (New York: G.P. Putnam's Sons, 1928), 610.

12. Dale Cyrus Wheary, "Swannanoa: Summer Home of James and Sallie Dooley, 1913–1925," *Augusta County Historical Bulletin*, vol. 50 (Staunton, Va.: Augusta County Historical Society, 2014), 19–34.

13. Sallie Dooley to Biltmore Nursery, February 19, 1912, Biltmore Estate Archives. Courtesy of Bill Alexander of Biltmore Estate.

14. *Richmond Times-Dispatch*, August 5, 1910, 5. The author wishes to thank Evelyn Zak for sharing this and many period newspaper articles quoted in this text.

15. "James H. Dooley," *Catholic Virginian*, vol. 7, no. 1 (November 1931), 15–16.

16. "Public Gifts Totaling $2,000,000 Included in Mrs. S. M. Dooley's Will, Biggest Ever Made by a Virginia Woman," *Richmond Times-Dispatch*, September 14, 1925.

17. City Hostess Day Book, February 22, 1926. Maymont Mansion Archives.

18. James H. Dooley, Testimony, Annexation Hearing Transcript, City of Richmond vs. Henrico County, 1906, 1813. Maymont was annexed into the city by sections in 1906 and 1914.

19. John E. Wells and Robert E. Dalton, *The Virginia Architects, 1835–1955* (Richmond: New South Architectural Press, 1997), 387–88. Rogers was also engaged by tobacco tycoon Lewis Ginter to transform Westbrook, his Richmond country place (demolished in 1975).

20. The City of Richmond replaced the mansion's original red slate roof with gray Buckingham slate in 1962.

21. Kenneth L. Ames, Maymont National Endowment for the Humanities Interpretive Self-Study Report, 1996.

22. Laurie Ossman, *Great Houses of the South* (New York: Rizzoli, 2010), 212.

23. "Brilliant Reception," *The Times* (Richmond), February 10, 1898, 5.

24. Richard Guy Wilson, interview, "Garden Estates," *America's Castles*, A&E Television Network, 1996.

25. "Mrs. Dooley's Brilliant Reception," *Richmond Dispatch*, February 13, 1898.

26. Miles Chappell, "Bernini and Francesco Grassia's 'Allegory of Human Life': The Origins and Clarification of Some Erroneous Suppositions," *Southeastern College Art Conference Review* (1983), 126–34. See also Jean-Paul Mazaroz, *Un Artiste et Amateur Éclairé au temps de Courbet* (Lons-le-Saunier: Musée des Beaux-Arts de Lons-le-Saunier, 2003).

27. Robert F. Doares, "On the Trail of a Canadian Dinner Service in the President Hayes Design," *American Ceramic Circle Journal*, vol. 18 (2015).

28. "Elegant Dinner Party," *Richmond Times-Dispatch*, February 14, 1904.

29. *Richmond Times-Dispatch*, December 7, 1912, 5.

30. Dale Cyrus Wheary, "Vanity of Vanities: A Tiffany and Company Rediscovery," *The Magazine Antiques* (April 2008), 102–03.

31. As the architect's floor plans did not survive, current understanding of the original use of the Cherry Room, the East Bedroom Suite, and the third floor is based on oral tradition, physical evidence, and floor plans of similar houses of the period.

32. Elizabeth L. O'Leary, *From Morning to Night: Domestic Service in Maymont House and the Gilded Age South* (Charlottesville: University of Virginia Press, 2003), 21, 36.

33. Ibid., 107, 111–17.

34. Ibid., 17.

35. Ibid., 119.

36. Ibid., 3–4.

37. Dooley, Testimony, Annexation Hearing Transcript, 1906, 1814–15.

38. The fall line is the geologic, north-south transition zone that separates the flat tidal region from the foothill region. It is most prominently displayed where a river crosses it. At Richmond the James River descends about one hundred feet over a span of seven miles with rapids and rock outcroppings both in the river and along its banks. East of Richmond, the James becomes navigable, flowing down to merge with other rivers near the mouth of the Chesapeake Bay.

39. Dooley, Testimony, Annexation Hearing Transcript, 1906, 1814.

40. "May Mont's Beautiful Roses," *Richmond Dispatch*, May 21, 1901, 6.

41. *Richmond Dispatch*, June 10, 1900, 18.

42. "Lovely Gardens: Expense Held Secondary in Building Park," *Richmond Times-Dispatch*, July 9, 1933, sec. 5, 3. The Dooleys promoted Taliaferro to estate manager in 1899. They stipulated in their wills that he be retained by the city in this capacity and allowed to occupy the Gatehouse after their deaths.

43. Wheary, "Swannanoa."

44. Mrs. Henry Coleman Baskerville, interview, April 1986.

45. "Italian Gardens at Home of Maj. J. H. Dooley: Landscape Gardeners Make Beautiful Picture at Maymont," *Richmond Times-Dispatch*, October 12, 1908.

46. James Dooley to Florence Dooley Lewis, April 11, 1913. Adele Clark Papers, Special Collections, James Branch Cabell Library, Virginia Commonwealth University, Richmond.

47. The author wishes to thank Calder Loth for identifying the design source for both the Cascade and Fountain Court.

48. "Maymont," *Richmond Times-Dispatch*, May 2, 1935. See also Fitzhugh Elder, Jr., interview, January 26, 1981. Elouise Binns and Bian Tan, "The Search for Muto" (unpublished paper, Morris Arboretum Archives, 1988). Clay Lancaster, *The Japanese Influence in America* (New York: Abbeville Press, 1983), 198.

49. Kendall H. Brown, *Quiet Beauty: Japanese Gardens in North America*, rev. 2nd edn. (Tokyo: Tuttle Publishing, 2013), 33.

50. The James River and Kanawha Canal Company formed in 1835 to provide transportation around the falls of the James and to connect with the Kanawha River and ultimately the Ohio and Mississippi Rivers. When railroads put the canal out of business, the Richmond and Alleghany Railroad bought the canal property and laid tracks on the towpath. The Chesapeake and Ohio (now CSX) purchased it around 1888. The canal and tracks form the southern boundary of Maymont and beyond it the James River.

51. Dooley, Testimony, Annexation Hearing Transcript, 1906, 1812–38.

52. After the Dooleys' time, the Work Projects Administration (WPA) added an extension to the building in addition to Stable Row and the granite wall enclosing the south side of the stable yard.

53. Mrs. James Robert Layne Fitzgerald, Sr., interview, March 24, 1976.

54. "The Sleigh Bells, A Carnival of the Snow," *Richmond Dispatch*, February 7, 1886. "Major Dooley's Fine Horse," *Richmond Dispatch*, December 12, 1902, 12. Mary Lynn Bayliss, "The Floral Carriage Festival, Historically Speaking," *Maymont Foundation Newsletter* (Fall 1996).

55. See n. 47.

56. Calder Loth, "The Dooley Mausoleum at Maymont," *Maymont Notes*, no. 2 (2002), 4–7.

57. Nancy Finch, "Dooley Museum is City's Albatross," *Richmond Times-Dispatch*, June 28, 1970.

Text and photography copyright
© Maymont Foundation 2015
Book copyright © Scala Arts Publishers, Inc. 2015

First published in 2015 by
Scala Arts Publishers, Inc.,
141 Wooster Street, Suite 4D,
New York NY 10012, USA
www.scalapublishers.com

in association with
Maymont Foundation
1700 Hampton Street
Richmond, VA 23220, USA
www.maymont.org

Distributed outside of Maymont in the booktrade by
ACC Distribution
6 West 18th Street, 4th Floor
New York, NY 10011, USA

ISBN (hardback): 978-1-85759-973-2
ISBN (paperback): 978-1-85759-974-9

Designed by Inglis Design
Copy edited by Nancy Eickel
Printed in China

10 9 8 7 6 5 4 3 2 1

Set in Adobe Centaur type designed by Bruce Rogers and produced by the Monotype Corporation Ltd. in 1929.

Maymont's trademarks are registered in US Patent and Trademark Office.

All rights reserved. No part of the contents of this book may be reproduced, stored in a retrieval system or transmitted in any form or by any means, electronic, mechanical, photocopying, recording or otherwise, without the written permission of the Maymont Foundation and Scala Arts Publishers, Inc. Every effort has been made to acknowledge correct copyright of images where applicable. Any errors or omissions are unintentional and should be notified to the Publisher, who will arrange for corrections to appear in any reprints.

Library of Congress
Cataloging-in-Publication Data

Wheary, Dale Cyrus.
 Maymont, an American estate / Text by Dale Cyrus Wheary.
      pages cm
 Includes bibliographical references.
 ISBN 978-1-85759-973-2 (hardback : alk. paper)—ISBN 978-1-85759-974-9 (pbk. : alk. paper)
 1. Maymont Park (Richmond, Va.) 2. Dooley, James H. (James Henry), 1841–1922—Homes and haunts—Virginia—Richmond. 3. Dooley, Sallie May—Homes and haunts—Virginia—Richmond. 4. Mansions—Virginia—Richmond. 5. Richmond (Va.)—Buildings, structures, etc. I. Title.
 F234.R57M399 2015
 975.5'451—DC23

                              2015022665

Photo and Illustration Credits:
(t: top; b: bottom; l: left; r: right; c: center)

Front cover, pp. 45, 52b, 58, 60t: Scott Strimple; back cover, front flap, pp. 3, 5, 7b, 8t, 44, 46t, 48, 51, 52tl, 53, 59t, 68, 69t, 70b, 73tr, 74c, 74b, 75tl, 75tr, 76r: Carla Murray; back flap, pp. 15, 18, 20, 21, 22, 23, 25, 27tl, 27br, 28, 29, 32, 34, 35, 36, 37, 46b, 47t: Dale Quarterman; p. 1: Robert Llewellyn; pp. 2, 14l, 24tl, 24bl, 26l, 27tl, 27c, 30, 31tr, 31br, 33, 40, 41t, 42t, 43, 71: Dennis McWaters; p. 6: Melanie Weyer; p. 7t: Betty Maxey; p. 8b, 61t, 64, 67l: Maymont Foundation; p. 9b: Jean Lua; pp. 9t, 49tl, 67r: Dale Wheary; pp. 10, 62, 77: Jay Paul; p. 12t: Dementi-Nolan; p. 12b, 16t, 17t, 42b, 59c, 59b, 60b, 61b, 65t: Maymont Mansion Collection; p. 13: Dementi Studios; p. 14r, 47b: Library of Virginia; p. 16b, 66t, 66b: The Valentine; p. 19: Richard Cheek; p. 24tr, 31tl: Katherine Wetzel; p. 26r: Gary Crallé; p. 38: Private Collection; p. 39: Harold P. Bailey; p. 41b: Doris Walker Woodson; p. 49tr, 54, 70t, 74t, 75b: Kevin Kelley; p. 49b, 73b: Skip Rowland; p. 50t: Tracey Crehan Gerlach; p. 50b: Kate Prunkl; p. 52tr: Victoria Robinson; p. 55: Candace Crawford; p. 56bl: John A. Cook; p. 56br: Nancy Fabian; p. 56t: Carol Haley; p. 57t: Michael Mancuso; p. 57b: Phoebe Reid; p. 63: Calder Loth; p. 65b: Julia Seay; p. 69b: Memories by PJ; p. 72: Danny Tiet; p. 73t: Kelly Armentrout; p. 73c: Rich Young; p. 76c: Haden Edwards III; p. 76b: Fred Murray; p. 76t: John Votta

Estate Map

MAYMONT
MAYMONT.ORG